Aigues-Mortes Travel Tips (France)

Discover the most up-to-date and amazing places to explore in Aigues-Mortes, along with current information and guides on when to go, what to do, and the best places to see.

Hudson Miles

All rights reserved. No part of this publication may be reproduced, distributed, or transmitted in any form or by any means, including photocopying, recording, or other electronic or mechanical methods, without the prior written permission of the publisher, except in the case of brief quotations embodied in critical reviews and certain other noncommercial uses permitted by copyright law.

Copyright © Hudson Miles), (2023).

Table Of Contents

Aigues-Mortes 101, Homie - A Peek into Aigues-Mortes's Secrets.

Chapter 2
Talk Like a Local, Holmes - Phrases and Slang Terms for Mixing In.

Chapter 3
Crash Pads in Aigues-Mortes - Where to Chillax in Style.

Chapter 4
Feasting Frenzy, Buddy - Area Cuisine and Dining Adventures.

Chapter 5
Must-See Aigues-Mortes: No Joke - Check Out the Coolest Spots.

Chapter 6
Shop 'n' Stop, My Friend - Retail Therapy Aigues-Mortes-Style.

Chapter 7
Let's Play, Aigues-Mortes - Leisure Activities for the Fun-Loving Traveler.

Chapter 8
Party Time in Aigues-Mortes, Y'all - Festivals and Events Galore.

Chapter 9
Route 'n' Roll - Rock Your Travels with Unique Itineraries

Self-Reflection questions

This travel guide provides helpful information. The ideas in the Day trips, Excursions, leisure activities, Itineraries in the city, and Neighboring cities are suggestions. You can craft and explore your vacation in your own style and preparation.

The attractions are listed with their opening hours, starting from the popular ones to the less-known ones. The map in this book provides some knowledge of the city, but the maps on your phone are more detailed. Consider taking screenshots as you walk around with no connection needed. Alternatively, you can contact the tourist office using the addresses and numbers provided in this guide.

If you have more time, explore both popular and less-known attractions mentioned in the notes below. Additionally, if you're interested in shopping, reach out to the stores or reach them through the contact numbers in this book.

For first timers, visiting or contacting the Tourist office, helps you get familiar with the city and it's attractions.

Lastly, try the travel prompts; they help enrich your travel experience and open avenues for personal growth.

The humor in the table of contents is included for an enjoyable reading experience.

Safe Trip....

The mediaeval Aigues-Mortes is where the Camargue gets its name. The tower of Constance, which was constructed in accordance with St. Louis's wishes, continues to be among the most imposing towers of mediaeval architecture. A Camarguaise gastronomic centre is surrounded by walls. Rust octopus, gardianne and bull flesh, aioli, anchoade, focaccia sugar, and wine sands are some of the restaurant's specialties.

Aigues-Mortes, the first Mediterranean port of the French monarchy, was established in the 13th century by Saint Louis with the intention of fostering trade with Italy and the Far East. It now exhibits a remarkably well-preserved variety of architectural styles. The settlement of Aigues-Mortes, located in the Gard Camargue, has the appearance of a genuine mediaeval stronghold thanks to its 1,634 metres of ramparts, defended gateways, twenty towers, and wall-walk. The Constance Tower, a former prison that is 30 metres high and the tallest building in Aigues-Mortes, provides a stunning view of the broad Camargue from its terrace.

Be sure to visit the Place Saint-Louis plaza inside the walls, which features a fountain topped with a statue of Saint Louis, as well as restaurant patios and stores.

Continue your exploration of the city walls to find the Gothic Notre-Dame-des-Sablons cathedral and the two Baroque structures known as the Chapel of the White Penitents and the Chapel of the Grey Penitents.

Tourist Information Centre Phone: +33 4 66 53 73 00 Address: BP 23 Pl. Saint-Louis, 30220 Aigues-Mortes, France

Day trips and Excursions

Below are suggestions on day trips and excursions, Embark on any of them to make your travel more enjoyable.

- Pope's Palace and Wine Option on the Avignon Walking Tour

Immerse yourself in Avignon's history with a competent guide. - Type: Historical Tours - Duration: 3-9 hours. Discover the Pope's Palace and benefit from insider knowledge
Cost: $60 for each adult.

- Food & Drink: Chateauneuf de Pape Wine Tour

- Time: 6 hours and more With a local guide who holds a Sommelier diploma, explore the renowned Chateauneuf du Pape vineyard.
Cost: $177 for each adult.

- From Avignon, the Best of Luberon in an Afternoon

On this half-day journey through Provence from Avignon, discover rural France and its breathtaking surroundings. - Type: Historical Tours - Duration: 5-6 hours.
Cost: $82 for each adult.

- Provence Wines over a Half Day: Châteauneuf-du-Pape, Gigondas...
 - Type: Food & Beverage
 Experience the flavours of Provence with a wine tour that includes a picnic with seasonal local fare. - Length: 5–6 hours.
Cost: $96 for each adult.

- A Day in Provence Day trip for a small group from Avignon
 Visit UNESCO monuments and mediaeval towns while taking a small-group tour of the Provençal region. - Type: Historical Tours - Duration: 6+ hours.
Cost: $142 for each adult.

Plan and Pack

Research and Itinerary: Start by learning about the fascinating history and cultural attractions of Aigues-Mortes. Make sure there is a good mix of historical places, regional cuisine, and leisure activities when planning your schedule.

The best seasons to travel to Aigues-Mortes are spring (April to June) and autumn (September to October). The excellent weather and reduced visitor traffic make for a more personal encounter.

Opt for lodgings that capture the beauty of the area. Aigues-Mortes provides a variety of lodging choices, including lovely bed and breakfasts and boutique hotels inside the city walls.

Transportation: To conveniently tour the nearby areas, think about renting a car. The town of Aigues-Mortes is well connected, so having a vehicle gives you freedom.

Must-Have Packing List: - Comfy shoes for strolling over cobblestone streets.

- Clothing that is breathable and lightweight for the Mediterranean climate.

- A hat and sunscreen for sun protection on sunny days.

- An electrical outlet adaptor for your electronic devices.

- Travel handbook for insights when travelling.

Must-See Attractions: Scale the mediaeval walls for sweeping panoramas.

- Investigate the Constance Tower and discover Aigues-Mortes' past.
- Explore the Place Saint-Louis for quaint shops and cafes.

Indulge in regional specialties like shellfish and fougasse.

- Shop for local delicacies and fresh products in the thriving markets.

Learn some fundamental French phrases. The locals will appreciate your attempts to learn and use their language and culture.

You'll be happy to know that our new travel guide includes all the details you require. Have fun travelling to Aigues-Mortes!

Chapter 2

Basic french phrases and area slang terms to know before travelling.

- Bonjour (Hello)
- Bonsoir (Good evening)
- Merci (Thank you)
- S'il vous plaît (Please)
- Excusez-moi (Excuse me)
- Oui (Yes)
- Non (No)
- Comment ça va ? (How are you?)
- Parlez-vous anglais ? (Do you speak English?)
- Pouvez-vous m'aider ? (Can you help me?)
- Où est... ? (Where is...?)
- Combien ça coûte ? (How much does it cost?)
- L'addition, s'il vous plaît (The check, please)
- Pouvez-vous répéter, s'il vous plaît ? (Can you repeat, please?)
- Je ne comprends pas (I don't understand)
- Excusez-moi, où sont les toilettes ? (Excuse me, where are the toilets?)
- Pouvez-vous prendre une photo de moi, s'il vous plaît ? (Can you take a photo of me, please?)
- J'aimerais réserver une table pour deux (I would like to reserve a table for two)
- Quelle heure est-il ? (What time is it?)

- Je voudrais acheter ceci (I would like to buy this)
- Où puis-je trouver un distributeur automatique ? (Where can I find an ATM?)
- Quel est le meilleur moyen de se rendre à... ? (What is the best way to get to...?)
- Avez-vous des recommandations pour un bon restaurant ? (Do you have recommendations for a good restaurant?)
- Pouvez-vous me donner l'adresse de... ? (Can you give me the address of...?)
- Est-ce que le service est inclus ? (Is service included?)
- Pouvez-vous me recommander un plat typique ? (Can you recommend a typical dish?)
- C'est délicieux ! (It's delicious!)
- Pouvez-vous me dire plus sur l'histoire de cette région ? (Can you tell me more about the history of this region?)
- J'ai une réservation au nom de... (I have a reservation under the name of...)
- Puis-je avoir l'addition, s'il vous plaît ? (Can I have the check, please?)
- Quand est l'heure de fermeture ? (When is closing time?)
- C'est magnifique ! (It's beautiful!)
- Où puis-je prendre un taxi ? (Where can I find a taxi?)

- Pouvez-vous recommander un bon endroit pour prendre un café ? (Can you recommend a good place for coffee?)
- Pouvez-vous m'indiquer le chemin vers la gare ? (Can you direct me to the train station?)
- Où puis-je acheter des souvenirs ? (Where can I buy souvenirs?)
- Quel est le mot pour... en français ? (What is the word for... in French?)
- À votre santé ! (Cheers!)
- C'est trop cher (It's too expensive)
- Je suis perdu(e) (I am lost)
- Pouvez-vous m'expliquer comment aller à... ? (Can you explain how to get to...?)
- J'ai une allergie à... (I am allergic to...)
- C'est fantastique ! (It's fantastic!)
- Pouvez-vous me recommander un endroit pour écouter de la musique ? (Can you recommend a place to listen to music?)
- Où puis-je trouver un bureau de change ? (Where can I find a currency exchange office?)
- Avez-vous des plats végétariens ? (Do you have vegetarian dishes?)
- Est-ce que vous acceptez les cartes de crédit ? (Do you accept credit cards?)
- Je voudrais essayer quelque chose de typiquement français (I would like to try something typically French)

- Merci beaucoup ! (Thank you very much!)

Slang terms
- Salut (Hi/Hello)
- Bouquin (Book, referring to a smart person)
- Trop cool (Too cool)
- La bagnole (The car)
- Fringues (Clothes)
- Chouette (Cool/Nice)
- C'est ouf ! (It's crazy!)
- Bosser (To work)
- Pote (Friend)
- Péter un câble (To lose one's temper)
- Kiffer (To like/enjoy)
- Bouffer (To eat)
- Taf (Job)
- Casse-pieds (Annoying)
- Baraque (House)
- Zut alors ! (Darn!/Oops!)
- Truc de ouf (Crazy thing)
- Pépère (Easy/Chill)
- Se marrer (To laugh)
- Flipper (To be scared)
- Flic (Police officer)
- Roupiller (To nap)
- Se planter (To make a mistake)
- Zizou (Nickname for Zinedine Zidane, may refer to skillful moves)

- Bof (Meh)
- Pénible (Annoying)
- Kif-kif (Same, same)
- Plouc (Country bumpkin)
- Boulangerie (Bakery; commonly used for a girl who looks good)
- Casser la tête (To annoy)

Chapter 3

Hotels

Below are recommended hotels to take note of; Consider booking your hotel in advance; Online travel websites like Trivago.com and Booking.com can assist.

Boutique Hotel des Remparts & SPA
   Location: 6 Pl. Anatole France
   Phone: +33 4 66 53 82 77
   Stylish 18th-century hotel, fine-dining restaurant, bar, and free breakfast in a historic setting.

Hotel Canal Aigues-Mortes
   Location: 440 Rte de Nîmes

Phone: +33 4 66 80 50 04

1950s property with stylish rooms, outdoor pool, free Wi-Fi, and parking convenience.

Hotel Restaurant Le Saint Louis
   Location: 10 Rue Amiral Courbet
   Phone: +33 4 66 53 72 68

   Cozy hotel offering simple rooms, free Wi-Fi, and a tapas restaurant with a charming garden terrace.

La Villa Mazarin
   Location: 35 Bd Gambetta
   Phone: +33 4 66 73 90 48

   Classically styled rooms in a villa, featuring an outdoor pool, hot tub, steam room, and gardens.

Hôtel Les Templiers
      Location: 21 et 23 rue de la republique, Bd Intérieur N
      Phone: +33 4 66 53 66 56

   Laid-back guesthouse with informal rooms, pool, courtyard, bar, and a bistro for a relaxed stay.

Hôtel Noemys - Aigues Mortes
   Location: 939 Rte de Nîmes
   Phone: +33 4 66 53 66 40

      Simple rooms, seasonal outdoor pool, and a low-key restaurant for a comfortable stay.

Hôtel Le Médiéval
  Location: 221 Av. Pont de Provence
  Phone: +33 4 66 53 76 48
  Casual rooms with free WiFi in a low-key hotel with an outdoor pool and optional buffet breakfast.

Hôtel Restaurant Le Mas Des Sables - Aigues-Mortes
  Location: CD979, Mas Cambon Route de Saint Laurent d'Aigouze
  Phone: +33 4 66 53 79 73
  Tranquil seasonal hotel in a park, offering casual quarters, outdoor pool, and a delightful restaurant.

Maison des Croisades
  Location: 2 Rue du Port
  Phone: +33 4 66 53 67 85
  Unassuming quarters in a simple hotel with a garden, complimentary parking, and Wi-Fi.

Hôtel Chez Carrière
  Location: 18 Rue Pasteur
  Phone: +33 4 66 53 73 07
  Unfussy lodging offering simple rooms, a restaurant, shaded terrace, and free Wi-Fi for a comfortable stay.

Chapter 4

Restaurants

Try any of the best restaurants for a relaxed and enjoyable time below, along with their contact details.

Le Dit-Vin
   Location: 6 Rue du 4 Septembre
   Phone: +33 4 66 53 52 76
   Rustic-chic venue for French classics with a cozy ambiance.

Le Saint Amour
   Location: 5 Rue Sadi Carnot

Phone: +33 9 81 17 91 61
Exquisite dine-in experience with French culinary delights.

Restaurant l'Atelier de Nicolas
Location: 28 Rue Alsace Lorraine
Phone: +33 4 34 28 04 84
Culinary craftsmanship in a charming setting.

Restaurant Le Duende
Location: 16 Rue Amiral Courbet
Phone: +33 4 66 51 79 28
Vibrant atmosphere, opens evenings with Spanish-inspired delights.

Restaurant Le Galion
Location: 24 Rue Pasteur
Phone: +33 4 66 53 86 41
French elegance by the canal, offering a refined dining experience.

Restaurant Aromatik - Cuisine Bistronomique
Location: 9 Rue Alsace Lorraine
Phone: +33 4 66 53 62 67
Modern French fusion, a culinary adventure for the senses.

Boem
Location: 253 Av. Pont de Provence
Phone: +33 4 34 28 42 30

Trendy hotspot, where culinary innovation meets a vibrant social scene.

Le Feu ô Plumes
   Location: 40 Av. Frédéric Mistral
   Phone: +33 4 66 93 83 55
   Fusion of fire and feathers, offering French delicacies with flair.

Le Bistrot Paiou
   Location: 1 Rue du 4 Septembre
   Phone: +33 4 66 71 44 95
   Traditional French bistro, a local favorite for hearty meals.

Ni vu, ni connu
   Location: Rue du Port
   Phone: +33 7 71 94 30 29
   Coastal charm, specializing in exquisite seafood dishes.

Restaurant Le Café Du Commerce
   Location: 11 Pl. Saint-Louis
   Phone: +33 4 66 53 71 71
   Historic ambiance, serving culinary delights in a timeless setting.

La table de Paco

Location: 10 Rue Marceau
Phone: +33 4 66 53 69 11
French elegance meets avant-garde flavors.

Restaurant Des Voyageurs
Location: 8 Pl. Saint-Louis
Phone: +33 4 66 53 60 77
Culinary journey with global flavors in a cozy atmosphere.

escargot

Chapter 5

Attractions

Below are some of the Attractions in the city, both the popular and the less-known ones, with their operating hours. Visit any of them, depending on your preference.

- Gardette Gate

Location: Pl. Anatole France

Hours: Open 24 hours

Iconic medieval gate welcoming visitors to historic Aigues-Mortes.

- Towers and Walls of Aigues-Mortes

Location: Logis du gouverneur, Pl. Anatole France

Hours: 10 am–5:30 pm

Medieval city defenses offering panoramic views of Aigues-Mortes.

- Le petit train des salins d'Aigues Mortes

Location: Aigues-Mortes, France

Hours: 10 am–6 pm

Discover the saltpans and natural beauty with a charming train ride.

- Constancy Tower

Location: Logis du Gouverneur, Pl. Anatole France
Hours: 10 am–5:30 pm

Historic tower offering a glimpse into Aigues-Mortes' medieval past.

- Carnet d'escales

Location: Bureau du port, 27 Quai des Croisades
Hours: 9 am–8 pm

Harbor office offering maritime services in a scenic waterfront setting.

- The Center for National Monuments

Location: Pl. Anatole France
Hours: 10 am–7 pm

Promoting and preserving national heritage within Aigues-Mortes.

- Maison du Grand Site de France de la Camargue Gardoise

Location: Rte Du Mole

Explore a wild trail, admire flamingos, and embrace nature's beauty.

- Happy Tour Aigues Mortes

Location: Saint-Laurent-d'Aigouze, France
Hours: 8 am–7 pm

On-site and online services for a joyful exploration experience.

- Salin d'Aigues-Mortes
Location: Route du Grau du Roi
Hours: 9:30 am–7:30 pm
Experience French salt production with an informative tour.

- Embankments Gate
Location: Bd Intérieur O
Hours: 10 am–5:30 pm
Historical gate offering access to Aigues-Mortes' charming embankments.

- Notre-Dame des Sablons Church
Location: Pl. Saint-Louis
Hours: 9 am–6 pm
Architectural gem, a place of worship in the heart of Aigues-Mortes.

- Musée Du Sel
Location: Route du Grau du Roi
Hours: 10 am–6:30 pm
A museum showcasing the beauty and history of salt production.

Chapter 6

Shopping

Below are some of the best shops in the city.
Try shopping in any of them and bring back some souvenirs home.

- Galerie Commerciale Saint Louis

Type: Shopping Mall
Address: 2 Rue Theaulon
Phone: +33 6 60 67 54 97

Diverse shopping destination, opens at 10 am for retail therapy.

- Après la Plage

Type: Women's Clothing Store

Address: 23 Rue Emile Jamais

Phone: +33 6 16 34 68 71

Fashion haven for women, opens at 10 am with delivery options.

- La Boutique

Type: Leather Goods Store

Address: 22 Rue de la République

Phone: +33 6 09 20 82 42

Elegance in leather, doors open at 10:30 am.

- Zeeman Aigues-Mortes

Type: Clothing Store

Address: 582 Rue des Marchands

Phone: +33 4 30 31 00 09

Fashion finds for all, opening at 9:30 am.

- Lacoste

Type: Clothing Store

Address: Gd Rue Jean Jaurès

Designer polos with iconic crocodile logos.

- Hexagone

Type: Leather Goods Store

Address: 6 Rue Victor Hugo

Phone: +33 4 66 53 76 26

Crafted leather elegance beckons, opens at 10 am.

- Galet-Des–volcans-Aigues-Mortes

Type: Health and Beauty Shop
Address: 25 Rue Emile Jamais
Phone: +33 6 98 98 50 45

Wellness essentials, opening at 10 am on Wednesdays.

- Coll Sophie

Type: Novelty Store
Address: 15 Rue de la République
Phone: +33 4 66 53 83 83

Unique finds to brighten your day.

- United-S

Type: Clothing Store
Address: 7 Rue Emile Jamais
Phone: +33 6 13 25 20 03

Fashion with convenience, offering kerbside pickup.

- Coton House

Type: Clothing Store
Address: 5B Gd Rue Jean Jaurès
Phone: +33 4 66 53 64 09

Comfortable and stylish clothing, opens at 10 am.

- Maripop's La Boutique

Type: Gift Shop
Address: 22 Rue de la République
Phone: +33 6 10 22 64 83
Unique gifts await, opening at 10:15 am.

- Blacks Legend - Aigues Mortes

Type: Clothing Store
Address: 6 Pl. Saint-Louis
Phone: +33 4 66 77 85 94
Fashionable choices for a stylish experience.

- Badiane

Type: Women's Clothing Store
Address: 11 Gd Rue Jean Jaurès
Chic selections for the modern woman.

- Castel

Type: Department Store
Address: 29 Gd Rue Jean Jaurès
Phone: +33 4 66 51 72 37
Wide-ranging choices for shoppers, opens at 10 am.

Chapter 7

Leisure Activities

Below are more activities and Excursions to get involved in.

4x4 Safari in the Wild Camargue - Enjoy the outdoors and nature in Aigues-Mortes for between $29 and $75 - Enjoy the thrill of a 4x4 safari through the Camargue, where you can see flamingos and explore a farmhouse from the 16th century that is surrounded by bulls and horses. positioned 820 metres from Aigues-Mortes's centre.

E-Ticket - Aigues-Mortes Towers and Ramparts - Culture and education in Aigues-Mortes - Cost: €8 - Visit Saint-Louis' ancient ramparts to take in the expansive vistas of the Camargue's salt marshes. Enjoy Aigues-Mortes' enchanting mediaeval atmosphere. situated 220 metres from Aigues-Mortes's centre.

Eco-tour of the Camargue in a Hydrogen 4x4 - Attraction at Le Grau-du-Roi - Cost: €25 to €49 - Set out on an environmentally friendly adventure with a former Camargue farmer, learning about regional customs, sustainable farming, and the Camargue's distinctive ecology. 5.8 kilometres away from Aigues-Mortes.

Carriage Ride in the Gard Camargue - Le Cailar's natural surroundings and outdoors - Cost: $15 to $60 - As you explore the Camargue's beautiful splendour, surrounded by nature, wildlife, and the calming sound of cicadas, take pleasure in the luxury of carriages. 12.3 kilometres away from Aigues-Mortes.

Horseback Ride in the Real Camargue - Enjoy the outdoors and nature in Le Grau-du-Roi - Cost: $30 to $90 - On horseback, quench your desire for freedom while discovering routes that are unavailable by other means and coming across flamingos and egrets. Fred and Annie served as hosts. 7.5 kilometres from Aigues-Mortes.

Sea and Camargue Cruise - La Grande-Motte Entertainment - Price: €8 to €15 - From April to November, take a sail on the "Obvious" of Étrave Croisière over the Mediterranean and the Camargue. Visits to Saintes-Maries-de-la-Mer and brunch or sunset aperitifs are two options. 8.7 kilometres away from Aigues-Mortes.

Canyoning in Hérault and the Montpellier Hinterland - Montpellier Sports Sensations - €40 - Dive into outdoor adventure with canyoning, via ferrata, climbing, hiking, and rappelling in the stunning surroundings surrounding Montpellier. Discover well-known locations like the Pic Saint Loup. 25 kilometres away from Aigues-Mortes.

Sports marvels at Saintes-Maries-de-la-Mer include sailing lessons. Price: between €75 and €160 The Camargue Nautique Club provides sailing instruction on a variety of boats, including catamarans and wingfoils. All skill levels welcome, with the option to rent equipment. 23 kilometres away from Aigues-Mortes.

The Crucial Pic Saint-Loup in Montpellier: regional cuisine for €75. Explore Pic Saint-Loup's renowned terroir on a half-day guided tour. Discover the art of winemaking while seeing two vineyards and savouring the flavours of Languedoc wines. 24 kilometres away from Aigues-Mortes.

Chapter 8

Festivals and events

Attending some of the events listed below in the city or nearby can help make your travelling memorable.

- International contemporary live performance during the Avignon Festival in July 2024. Experience cutting-edge live acts from around the world at the Avignon Festival, which will enthral audiences in the mediaeval city of Avignon.

- Chorégies in Orange—the oldest lyric art festival—will take place in July 2024 in Orange. Travel to Orange for Chorégies, the oldest lyric art festival in the Théâtre Antique, which will enchant audience members with classical and operatic performances.

- Arles Meetings, an international photography event that will take place there in July and September 2024. Arles Meetings, an international photography festival, will showcase visual storytelling while illuminating the city's ancient streets.

- St. Louis Festival, a historic water jousting competition, will take place in Sète in August 2024. Discover the bustling St. Louis Festival in the picturesque city of Sète, where water jousting competitions combine history and excitement.

- Pentecost Feria - A beloved tradition with thrilling bullfights and bull runs, capturing the energy of the community - May/June 2024 in Nîmes - Celebrate the Pentecost Feria in Nîmes, a traditional event with bullfights that captures the passion of the town.

- Easter Feria, an occasion focused on bullfighting, will take place in Arles in March 2024. Join the Arles Easter Feria, a bullfighting spectacular that draws thousands and combines history and excitement in the middle of the city.

- Nîmes Festival - Concerts in the Nîmes Arena - Nîmes, France, July 2024 Take part in the Nîmes Festival, a captivating series of performances that reverberate throughout the famed Nîmes Arena and offer a musical trip.

- Nîmes' Roman Days will feature the magic of Roman games in the arena in May 2024. At the Roman Days of Nîmes, travel back in time and take in the allure of the legendary Arena's ancient Roman sporting events.

- Montpellier Danse - Event in the world of new dance - June/July 2024 in Montpellier - Montpellier Danse celebrates the avant-garde and is a must-attend event for fans of contemporary dance. Montpellier will be filled with inventive and enthralling performances.

- What A Trip! "Heyme Festival": International Travel & Adventure, Montpellier, September 2024 At the Heyme Festival, a worldwide celebration of travel and adventure held in the dynamic city of Montpellier, set off on a voyage of discovery.

- The New Beaujolais Festival, a celebration of new Beaujolais wine, will take place from November 16 to 19, 2023, throughout France. Participate in the nationwide celebration at the New Beaujolais Festival, which marks the introduction of the new Beaujolais wine with events all around France.

- Enjoy a cultural evening at European Museum Night, a national event that invites you to learn about the rich history of museums across France. Festive evening of museum discovery, May 2024, everywhere in France.

- Rendez-vous aux Jardins Garden Festival – Gathering for plant and nature lovers – June 2024, all over France – Discover nature's splendour at Rendez-vous aux Jardins, a national garden festival for both animal and plant enthusiasts.

- World Music Day, a national celebration featuring a variety of musical genres, will take place on June 21, 2024, throughout France. Join in the harmony of World Music Day, a national celebration in France that offers a variety of musical genres for all audiences.

Chapter 9

Itinerary

Below is a detailed 6 days Itinerary suggestions, you can adjust it based on your preference and timing.

Day 1: Arrival and a Tour of the Past
- Morning: Get to Aigues-Mortes and find a place to stay.
- In the afternoon, start your tour of the area with a stroll through the city's ancient walls, beginning with the Constance Tower. Explore the town's historic ramparts to discover more about its colourful past.
- In the evening, savour a classic Provençal meal at a neighbourhood bistro.

Day 2: Take a Salt Marshes tour.
- In the morning, visit the enormous salt marshes of the Salins du Midi. Learn about the manufacture of salt and its importance to the area by taking a guided tour.
- In the afternoon, unwind at a salt pan and maybe even sample some of the renowned fleur de sel. For a different perspective of the wetlands, take a boat excursion.

- In the evening, eat supper while taking in the tranquil surroundings at a waterfront restaurant.

Day 3: Mediterranean boat trip
- In the morning, board a boat from Aigues-Mortes and go to the Mediterranean Sea. Discover the Camargue's natural splendour and discover the area's animals.
- In the afternoon, reach Le Grau-du-Roi, a seaside community. Go beach hopping, eat lunch by the harbour, and possibly sample some local cuisine.
- Return to Aigues-Mortes in the evening for a leisurely evening in the Old Town.

Day 4: Safari adventure in the Camargue
- In the morning, take a safari tour with a guide through the Camargue, a sizable natural reserve renowned for its distinctive flora and fauna. See flamingos, wild horses, and other bird species.
- In the afternoon, pay a visit to the historic citadel of Aigues-Mortes. Climb the tower for sweeping views of the Camargue.
- In the evening, eat dinner at a neighbourhood brasserie while sampling local delicacies.

Visit Saintes-Maries-de-la-Mer on day five.

- In the morning, travel quickly to the quaint beach town of Saintes-Maries-de-la-Mer. Visit the Camargue Museum and the fortified church.
- In the afternoon, unwind on the fine-sand beaches, meander through the charming streets, and perhaps stop by the neighbourhood market.
- In the evening, travel back to Aigues-Mortes for a final dinner at a fine dining establishment.

Sixth day: Departure
- Morning: Depending on when you leave, go for a leisurely stroll in Aigues-Mortes or finish off any unfinished souvenir purchases.
- Afternoon: Check out of your lodging and leave Aigues-Mortes, with pleasant Provencal memories.
Introduction:

Self-Reflection questions

Below are some personal questions, answering them can help enrich your travel experience. Safe trip

Self-reflection is an effective tool for travellers since it provides the chance to delve more deeply into one's own experiences and glean insightful information. Asking probing questions can help you gain a deeper knowledge of your journey, promoting personal development and improving the entire travel experience.

Prior to departure:

1. What do you hope to get out of this journey to France's Aigues-Mortes? What potential effects do you think these assumptions might have on how you view the location?

_____
_____
_____
_____
_____
_____
_____

2. Think about Aigues-Mortes' historical significance. What features of its past and present pique your interest the most, and why? How might knowing this historical background improve your trip?

_____
_____
_____
_____
_____
_____
_____

3. Consider your chosen travelling method. Do you like impulsive exploration or carefully thought-out itineraries? How might your time in Aigues-Mortes be affected by this preference?

_____
_____
_____
_____
_____
_____
_____

4. Consider how you want your travels to affect your personal development. During your stay at

Aigues-Mortes, what abilities or traits would you wish to hone?

_____
_____
_____
_____
_____
_____
_____

5. Keep the regional food in mind. What particular cuisines or flavours are you keen to sample, and how can these culinary explorations help you better comprehend the local way of life?

_____
_____
_____
_____
_____
_____
_____

After a trip:
1. Think back to the Aigues-Mortes experiences that most surprised you. How did these

unanticipated encounters affect your opinion of the place as a whole?

_____
_____
_____
_____
_____
_____
_____

2. Take into account your encounters with locals. What cultural insights did you obtain from these discussions, and how did they affect your understanding of the community?

_____
_____
_____
_____
_____
_____
_____

3. Consider the difficulties or discomforts you experienced while travelling. What did you discover

about your resilience and flexibility as a result of how you handled these circumstances?

_____
_____
_____
_____
_____
_____
_____
_____

4. Consider the monuments and historical sites you have seen. What personal meanings did these locations have for you, and what fresh insights into the past and culture of Aigues-Mortes did they provide?

_____
_____
_____
_____
_____
_____
_____
_____

5. Take into account how the surrounding environment affects your health. How did your sense of inspiration or tranquilly be affected by the natural surroundings, such as the salt marshes or the Mediterranean Sea? How could you use these advantageous aspects to your regular home life?

_____
_____
_____
_____
_____
_____
_____
_____

**Help leave positive reviews and check out other cities in France by the author.
"Hudson Miles"
Safe travels**

Note:

Note:

Note:

Note:

Printed in Great Britain
by Amazon